NEW ARCANA

Jessica Traynor was born in Dublin in 1984 and is a poet, essayist and librettist. Her debut collection, *Liffey Swim* (Dedalus Press, 2014), was shortlisted for the Strong/Shine Award and in 2016 was named one of the best poetry debuts of the past five years on Bustle.com. Her second collection, *The Quick*, was a 2019 *Irish Times* poetry choice. *A Place of Pointed Stones*, a pamphlet commissioned by Offaly County Council, was published by The Salvage Press in 2021. The poems were later featured in a radio programme written and presented by Jessica Traynor, *The Lyric Feature: A Place of Pointed Stones*, first broadcast on Lyric FM in 2023. Her third collection, *Pit Lullabies*, was published by Bloodaxe Books in 2022. It was a Poetry Book Society Recommendation and an *Irish Times* poetry books of the year choice for 2022, and was shortlisted for the inaugural Yeats Society Sligo's Poetry Prize in 2023. Her fourth, *New Arcana*, followed from Bloodaxe in 2025.

She has received commissions for poems from BBC Radio 4, The Arts Council of Ireland, The Model Gallery Sligo, The Salvage Press, VISUAL Carlow, Dún Laoghaire–Rathdown County Council and *The Poetry Programme* (RTÉ), and awards including the Hennessy New Writer of the Year, the Ireland Chair of Poetry Bursary, and the Listowel Poetry Prize. In 2016, she was named one of the 'Rising Generation' of poets by Poetry Ireland. She received the Lawrence O'Shaughnessy Award for Poetry 2023, and also the Field Day Tundish Award 2024, for contribution to the arts in Ireland.

She has reviewed poetry for *The Irish Times*, RTÉ Radio 1's *Arena*, and for *Poetry Ireland Review*. She was an inaugural Creative Fellow of UCD, where she completed her MA in Creative Writing in 2008, and has held residencies including the Yeats Society, Sligo, and Carlow College. She was Dún Laoghaire-Rathdown Writer in Residence for 2021-22 and University of Galway Writer in Residence for 2023. She is poetry editor at Banshee.

JESSICA TRAYNOR

NEW ARCANA

BLOODAXE BOOKS

Copyright © Jessica Traynor 2025

ISBN: 978 1 78037 749 0

First published 2025 by
Bloodaxe Books Ltd,
Eastburn,
South Park,
Hexham,
Northumberland NE46 1BS.

www.bloodaxebooks.com
For further information about Bloodaxe titles
please visit our website and join our mailing list
or write to the above address for a catalogue.

Supported using public funding by
ARTS COUNCIL
ENGLAND

Cover design: Lisa Sterle.

Printed in Great Britain by Bell & Bain Limited, 303 Burnfield Road,
Thornliebank, Glasgow G46 7UQ, Scotland, on acid-free paper
sourced from mills with FSC chain of custody certification.

I'm just as good as anybody
I'm just as bad as anybody

LUCY DACUS

I don't judge people,
I just watch them till it's time to look away

KRISTIN HERSH

No more Virgos

CMAT

CONTENTS

I

Again he measured a thousand, and brought me
through the waters; the waters were to the knees.
Again he measured a thousand, and brought me
through; the waters were to the loins

EZEKIEL 47:4

The Hive

XXIII

what the mirror told me –
a whole gash of bees
flying in to breed
and make honey
in the hole you left

Lydia...

Draw some cards for me, wherever you are.
I know we don't talk much these days
but I've been thinking about the time
you set your college dorm on fire
and came to live with us.
Now, I'm trying your tactics –
I set a fire inside myself.
It's cleared space and my halls
are black-lacquered & echoing. The problem is,
I don't like the new tenants.
Inside me is a great tall house,
all clapboard and dead ivy.
Why don't you and I play ghosts,
why don't you and I play girls no one can touch.
Draw three cards for me, tell me how it goes.

Bog Virgin

After The Butcher Boy *by Pat McCabe*

Once I walked the road in a blue dress
and a poet told me
I looked like the virgin mary,

so that was me then, stella maris
sitting with him in the seafood restaurant
eating chowder, clams and mussels

sluicing down my throat.
The poet told me I should write from my cunt
because paddy kavanagh never did

and look what happened to him.
Then he took me back to the bog,
told me to ignore the little men

crawling in apocalyptic clay –
keep your eye trained on the mystic beyond,
he said, forcing me onto my knees.

and if they hurt you, write your curses onto them
till they shrivel like salted slugs.
So there I was, kneeling in ditchwater,

writing hexes and levitating as required
but only when the sun came out,
which wasn't often. Today

I'm really here to say,
the bad world is out there, lydia,
pushing in around us

and packing up our lungs.
you'd better rub their slurry on your face
till you blend in because right now

I can see the devil in you a mile off –
can see it pulling up from within
some great bog leviathan,

trailing priests and poets
who want to drown us both
in its wet centre.

monstera

mum tells me i climbed up a wall of shelves to eat it
    and she thought i would die
      swiss cheese plant   lacquer-leaved threat
       i tasted curd in my mouth every time i spoke
          longed to pack my mouth with cheesecloth
     until my breath was a whisper through thread's chains
the wet in me all sucked away   oh my lost monstera
      guard the shadows of our house   haunt the corners
        twine your arms around me
           as i lick your poisoned wax
i'll take the chance to practise
      i've years of this ahead of me.

and the girl inside me

slides out and jerks up on her legs like a wet foal
and falls over for a man and drags herself through the streets
rattling like a string of cans
sweeps up leaves and dirt and pigeon feathers
in her hair

and the girl inside her shimmies out, makes a perfect dismount
but she staggers, and there's broken glass studding her legs –
and she's a car siren you can't knock off

and the girl inside her claws out
through pondweed
turf under her fingernails and she's *roaring*
but over she goes –

and the therapist says *I just*
want to stop
you there you know
that trauma isn't all that's passed on –

roaring I continue and over
she goes
over she
goes –

Satanic Panic

We are fourteen
and we are nothing
beyond ourselves.
You bring vodka into school –
Carla calls me flat-chested
and I call her a hairy-backed bitch.
When she hits me
you shove her so hard
that you fall backwards
and everyone laughs
except the head nun
who brings us to her office
where, reclined on the sofa,
she tells us about some teenagers
who crucified their neighbour
(and that we're not to do that).
Then we're off into the laneways
to hex all our enemies
with matches, tea lights, bottle-tops,
to be so present-tense.
Come collect a past with me –
I think we can make something
from all this broken glass.
I need you,
because every girl needs a friend who goes too far
every girl needs a friend who goes too
every girl needs a friend who goes
every girl needs a friend who
every girl needs a friend
every girl needs a
every girl needs

Roger Moore's Swimming Pool

When your mother married the bank manager,
she dragged you to a house in Dalkey
once owned by Roger Moore.
It was ugly, flat-roofed, but we were learning
that wealth and beauty don't marry –
beauty was not the point, the point
was an empty swimming pool,
and the whole house haunted by chlorine.
You were given a TV room – a subterranean lozenge
where I pictured a hundred monkeys
chained to typewriters, writing the next James Bond.
As a gift it was tundric in scope.
At your mother's fancy party we drank all the drink ends
then went downstairs and watched MTV.
I thought that the next logical step would be to kiss you,
but then I was puking in a bucket in your room.
When your mum came in to shout at me
the best revenge I could think of
for the chlorine, the school move,
the cuts all over your arms
was to shout she was a fucking poisoner
and that she had poisoned me
just like she'd poisoned you.

i'm lydia deetz and all my friends are dead

       thanks for welcoming me to the circle
i didn't think it would end like this. even though
       i asked for it by wearing black. by wearing a veil
(demon thirst trap) by hanging around
       this older man. i swear he had charisma.
ok. he saw me like no one else ever
       saw me. even if that means that he saw himself
in every mirror i looked into.
       someone has to mind the strays.
girls are so afraid of maggots. grave worms.
       black eyes.
what's in it for me? well, I'm still here.
       and I'm getting better. a lady in the chelsea market
read my aura, told me to trust my instinct, not my brain.
       how do i know which is talking? i asked.
the instinct doesn't negotiate, she said,
       the mind and its problems are all this red tulle –
she pointed to my wedding dress –
       this indigo light at your throat is the truth, she said,
running her fingers along my rope burn.

Lydia Reads the Cards

The Lovers / The King of Wands / The Queen of Swords

so   he wants you
the rock rises up between you   the angel
     looks away
         no landscape here that wouldn't
     break your ankles
no bed to lie in   but plenty of trees
to fuck against
no more wand jokes
         i'm just here on my throne
and my wrists are so tired
     from holding this big sword
         and his ankles are the only thing
you could damage
     you don't look me in the eye
         it's like that poem we read about leaves unfurling
     but you don't know what to do with yours
you could give him apples
you could give him worms

He Gets Her the Cloths of Heaven

What is this – what are *these* – were you painting? – I can't –
the door won't – *oh I see* – is that the – sorry, caught my foot –
is that a cloud – the moon? Weren't there silver apples? –
oh a different poem – why's it *yellow* there – half-light? Stars?
Mushroom clouds? The H-bomb's searing blink? Is this
the negative version? The halo you see inside your eyelids?
The anvil of sleep that refuses to drop?

                              ...where should we keep them? On the bed?

Of course they're beautiful – it's just –
other people's dreams are –
well –
other people's dreams.

                        I'm sorry I've walked dirt – oh –
                        I think it's dog shit –
                        right there beside the plough –
                        along the horizon too –

I'll try to be more careful –
maybe –
maybe let's just take these off the floor.

The Liar

XXIV

no form until he's up close
and then he's in you, fingers tangled
in your bronchioles.
How to pin him to this waxed card
when he keeps shifting shape.
How to shuffle the deck so that he won't lie there face up
asking you
to meet him where he ends.

Becoming Schrödinger's Cat

Consider me a cat as I run from you.
All cats look grey at night and all women
might be saying *yes* or at least thinking it.
They might be *yes*-ing and *no*-ing at the same time.
I said *no*, and you called me a cunt.
Recast the word as *cat*, watch me melt into the alley.
Cats vanish all the time and we think nothing of it –
it's their prerogative to be mysterious
even if that dusting of power is what gets them thrown
on bonfires, or strung up as the year thins.
As the sound of your shout dies in your throat
and anger shrivels to an apple core,
imagine me locked in a box.
            Keep me there, safe in the knowledge
that I'm alive, that I'm dead.

Ezekiel 47:11

Lydia, there's a man here
telling me my house is flooding –
the river in my hall's a giveaway I say.
He's talking about how the water will heal me,
with one hand on the small of my back,
the other cupping my skull,
as if he could fold me like a trestle table.
Everyone else in the world is asleep.
No one is seeing this; the cloud
tongue deep in the sea,
or the man in my house,
how he's holding my face as I cry.
If I collaged words from his big speech
I could make the sentence *i* ███████████████

███████████████████████ *need*

███████████ *you* ████████████████
You know me, lydia, I'll let him dunk me in the water
if he wants to. If it'll make him happy.
All those boys we knew. Now he's saying
the miry places and the marishes shall not be healed
and I can let them go, lydia – all the salted things that
can't be saved. Hold my hand, and promise me,
you'll keep your eyes open as we go under.

Queen of Cups

I *minor complaints*

the loneliness of never being alone
that you love me in spite of/
that you'll never love me
the right way
that i have all these surfeits
of incorrect love
like empty wineglasses
messing up my kitchen
someone please take
these coupes and flutes
and throw them
in the dirty sea
that slouches at the end of my road
heaving like a drunk
trying to rise from bed
there's a lesson here somewhere
i think as i chuck my excess
off the pier
only to see the tide's out
and all my crimes are glittering

II *raptured*

I'm thinking how water's the only element that loves a body –
can hold and be inside it at the same time
when the man appears
and maybe it's because of how I'm slumped on the bench
messaging you
my legs too wide apart
but he tells me how he fell in love with Jesus
and he simpers, hands clasped,
as he describes how we'll all be raptured
and he does a little trumpet sound: 'do-*DOO!*'
before he begins to pray over me
and I feel my legs creep shut as he talks about
the corrupted bodies in their graves.
how we'll swap them for brand new ones.
Liquefaction, I think, *putrefaction, dis-comp-o-si-tion*,
as he talks about how we'll all be Christ's brides
and this queer heaven doesn't sound too bad
except we'd all have to share one white guy
so I tell him if the rapture's coming
I've some things to get done,
and off I scurry, his voice
still lapping my back.
And even though the moment's wrecked
I find
he hasn't dammed the river
that you've sprung in me –
the only part still holding out against it
is my lungs.

III *mean/meant aubade*

If we were to try to keep this even,
or at least find the midpoint
in this argument
                  before anyone gets mean
we'd be golden.
Let's say when you said
       maybe we're not meant to be with just one person
       I had responded with –
— what do you mean by *being with someone*
— what do you mean by *meant*
       but instead, I swallowed
       the plumb-line you tossed and felt it pin me to the bed
       finding chamber
              within chamber within which, the seductive intersection
       of curve and right angle – *can't you understand what I mean?*
       Imagine this wasn't ending tonight. Imagine adders in a meadow
       coiling together in a trembling column
       until the female leaves, dragging the spent male in her wake.
Outside the window,
all things are coalescing to their natural order,
the light falling even as a fire curtain.
What was meant was said. You are comforted.
But I won't sleep for days
       the plumb-line's rising out of me now
crashing through every floor above us.

IV *THE PRIZE*

I let the word *insula* slip around my mouth like an oyster,
yes, like the oyster you said you would serve me
in a brand new converse trainer.
The oyster is a harbour – same colours, close up or far away,
same smell, same wetness – for me to dock my tongue.
And this harbour has an island attached –
you promise me an *insula*. Meaning island.
To insulate oneself – becoming island.
I wonder what kind. Will it have a well,
a house, or simply be
an outcrop on which my madness
will go unwitnessed?
I stand on this rock with my converse
and my oysters and I stare at the waves' crazing
at the black crucified forms of guillemots
on the far shore. It starts to rain.

>   *You would do all this for me?* I ask.
>   *No, for the Prize,* you say.

The Conductor

XXV

one flick of the wrist and he conjures
a solipsism so orchestral
it sounds like empathy.
Watch him. He thinks
the universe resolves
around him.

Movie Night with Lydia

I *Becoming Catwoman*

My mother was a secretary like Selina Kyle,
before Christopher Walken pushed her out a window –
(Selina, not my mother). My seven-year-old self
watches her body slam through awnings
(not my mother's body, but Selina's),
splatting onto Tim Burton's snowy alleyway.
Then the cats envelop her like the fur coat
that hung in the wardrobe at home, the one
she always said was suspiciously tabby-striped
(my mother, not Selina) and they lick and lick her
and somehow this reknits her shattered spine,
her arms and legs swivel into place, but her glasses,
her large owl-eye glasses (my mother's and Selina's)
are smashed and this is the worst, just the worst day –
pushed out the window! By a man with
a bad wig no one mentions because bosses
can look stupid while pushing women out of skyscrapers
and it's like, *ugh, bad day at the office.*
And up she gets and makes her way home
to her little girl apartment so we can see
she's just been playing at being a woman –
she's built herself a toyshop to get lost in,
(Selina, not my mother) and she splatters the walls
with black paint, smashing toys, and as a little girl
(me, not my mother, not Selina) this is just devastating,
because it feels like we aren't allowed
to have anything soft –
no knitted kittens or kit-cat klocks –
because it makes us weak and the only way to stop

men with Struwwelpeter hair
from pushing us out of skyscrapers
(me, my mother, Selina) is by killing
everything we love so that no one else can.

II *The Ice Princess Falls*

Cristi Conway who plays the Ice Princess
in *Batman Returns* says of her 'She's the type
to push an old lady down and try to fix her nail
at the same time.' On first read I'm confused –
she'd want to fix the old lady's nail? –
but that's not what she means.
My memory of her is all fox-fur corset
and obscene curls. All open mouth and eyes and tits.
She seems to be getting what she wants –
until she's kidnapped and then she's pure throat,
birthing this colt-scream,
body stretched like one of Bacon's popes
as she crashes through the Christmas tree
and bats swarm out, deranging the crowd.
Everyone is unhappy that this beautiful body is broken on the ground,
but things keep happening to pull the camera away.
There is a cautionary tale here, about the dangers
of being pretty and not very nice.
I rewind her fall from the base
of the Christmas tree so she hurtles upwards
into Batman's outstretched arms, but she won't stay put,
and the bats won't go back in the tree.

III *The Circus Performers' Desertion*

Pity the Penguin, poor Oswald Cobblepot,
emerging from sewers to a mansion
filled with ghosts of Waspish parents.

Who chooses to be a cautionary tale –
one that slurps fish heads at fundraisers,
until the surface-dwellers flush him again?

Underneath the zoo, emperor penguins glide,
back-lit, through an element
forgiving of bulk,

but as Batman cruises closer in the Batsub,
the Red Triangle Gang melt away.
The blonde who announces, deadpan,

that something is coming closer –
Very large. And very fast –
fades into the gloom behind set walls,

leaving us to ask if she was ever there?
And maybe Oswald never survived
his fall into the sewers, his ladder gone –

maybe men like this don't emerge
into the light after such damage
to hold our gaze

as they dribble chewed fish brains
from their lips?

IV *Things That Have Made Me Cry Today*

Michelle Pfeiffer
bullwhipping the heads
off four mannequins
in a single take
then using her whip
as a skipping rope
while the whole crew *(wow!)*
cheers.

V *Kissing Max Shreck*

I would like to tell you how it feels,
after all this waiting, to cup his face and kiss him.
These elver lips, this shock of hair,
the judder of his jawbone on my palm.
It's snowing sparks, they're dancing on the water.
A day comes when we all have
to give ourselves up to the current,
let the pain that lives bone-deep
spill into every cell. It's a flame in the brain,
along the tongue, from my mouth into his.
Can't you be happy for me?
It's snowing grease, his hair's on fire.
Don't look away until I'm finished.

Lydia Reads the Cards

The Seven of Pentacles / The King of Wands / The Ten of Pentacles

your staff is sprouting but my cornucopia
                           overflows
     i have gourds in every colour
i see you've shucked your skin again   still
               sucking on your tail.
i know candy's for daddies
              but don't worry, i'm the daddy
i'm the root that digs your core into earth
      i'm the lion passant
             paw clamped   on your lizard brain.

dear (name)

i'm saying *wait* juggling the baby and two bags
and you walk away
saying *wait* walking behind you when we're about to miss
the turn we need to take | we need to take this turn
the reasons I know are boring but I've thought them through
dear (name) please bend towards me
dear (name) please don't ask me to explain myself
tuesday spills like syrup
onto the counter
soon even the limescale remover will not shift it
soon the only method will be to gouge with a butter knife
and that exhausts the gift i've already given you
that seemed so infinite once –
it takes my fucking time.

*

dear (name)
i dreamed i pulled the wallpaper down
in one strip like a lizard's skin
i dreamed we bitched about artex
i dreamed i painted one pristine corner of architrave
the blackest blue i could find
and then cried over how
many coats of white
i would need to vanish it.

*

dear (name)
i wanted to say ████ to you
but ████ is not a word we can allow
in a poem and so here I try to concretise
its wan abstraction
i would say: the colour of the haze that leaches from a summer sky in evening
i would say: the heat of skin that's warmed to match the skin it touches
i would say: taste: strawberry juice. The hidden heart of lilac bushes.
the itch of grass against ankles. Its blade's serration splitting air into whistle.
i would say: let's swap the *o* for *ea*, and go.

*

dear (name)
i dreamed i was carrying lydia down the street
cradled like a tired child
when you passed
you asked me to come to dinner –
and you were so tall
your arms crosshatched with scars
and i thought you might be impressed
i was carrying my friend
who was crying inconsolably because
she had said she loved me and I'd told her
i loved her too, but not like that,
and that you might admire my strength
in picking up a woman my own age
but i could see from your face
you just thought it strange.

*

dear (name)
i spent the day on the bandstand under the sky at a ceremony
    in memory of the dead
under the blue blue sky (like we were viewing the oceans from above,
or fathoms of water from below) I thought of you
during the minute's silence when all sound dropped like ash i thought of you
imagined heaving my head from your waist
to your neck and settling down
like a beast for sleep
i felt each knot in my hair
i felt the sinew of your shoulder
flinch under my head's weight
i thought these things as the world dreamed of its dead, i confess it –
while the bandstand burned, the sky
stood blind above it.

*

dear (name)
if you say this stuff out loud
it just gets weathered
it can't be hurt if it's already dead
so sky-bury me –
here i am naked and rotten.

Your unifying theory of everything

i'm lying here in awe of you just
rattling it off
i see you build your tower of babel and i'm sliding helter-skelter down it
      — oh baby i'm outside like cathy! —
just let me in where i'll tear open
my wunderkammer
show you in each of my cabinets
sprawling bosch triptychs
bruegel landscapes
all pissy yellow
small tragedies unfolding in the margins
whole lives lost under ice
sucked back into amniotic sacs
where their tadpole brains
pulse in sync but cannot
form opinions –
how's that for negative capability
     motherfucker?

The Mistress

XXVI

of nothing but
the hollow
in his smallest
matryoshka doll.

The Tower

Lying awake, a fizzing on the plains
of my skull. I draw the tower

and feel the lightning enter me
cauterising as it goes

until my bat heart has no purchase
in the hole of my chest.

Underneath the cards' laminate the two
of us are falling, in flames.

We are burning and we are falling
and we are stuck.

The Marishes

In the slob lands, a vision:
Stoker, in bed at the crescent,
shakes in a fever dream.
Workmen at the crossroads
drive stakes into corpses
as the GAA Ticket van pulls up.
I'm tailing Joyce along Waterfall Avenue,
china clay clogging our shoe treads.
The bombed-out terraces
of the North Strand flicker
and I see the horizon,
threaded with *Newman's*
cloistral, silver-veined prose.
                              After dark,
you'll find me with Mangan
and all the other lip-stitched ghouls
loitering by the city wall
for a grave-digging job
at the old Jewish cemetery.
I'm deader than any of them –
thieves, thralls and hurlers.
While my children sleep, Lydia,
this is where I go – come visit
my posthumous hovel.
I'll pour you a Goldschlager.
We'll wait for your mother
to shake the grave-dirt from her car keys
and come to take you home.

I'm Quartered

like a Renaissance etching
where the body is divided
into little antechambers

with servants scuttling around –
their quaint hats!
Their whispered conversations!

They're bringing drinks on salvers
And plucking game, ignoring
my leaking ventricles.

Between my breast sits a throne
and in it, a bored angel
with a serpent and mace.

In the lower realms,
they've planted the acres
of my intestines

and set a crowd of serfs
to rotate the crops. The whole shebang
is a working demonstration

of women's mysterious innards,
where the servants argue
and spill the choler into the bile,

beat dust from my bed-curtain lungs.
Above and outside all of this,
my head alone escapes cross-section.

Does this point
to a tragic emptiness?
I have no faith in this kingdom,

except that I know the sun
must rise and set,
and sometimes I feel the rain.

Sheila on the Red Bed

after Patrick Graham

When we lie together on this bed,
I'm a paper lantern, blood galloping beneath my skin.
My face melds into my torso, which I hold open for you, yellow bittern –
come and drink from me, you'll be dead long enough.

The light permeates everything – against its walls
bones quail and bodies spatchcock.
In the darkest space, the heart, and tied to it
a bag to catch the loss.

Magpie

(for Victoria Kennefick)

What surprises me most about the egg cleanse is that every time I touch the egg to my heart I start to cry, and I find myself saying aloud *my poor heart!* like it's the chick from the egg hatched into a magpie, crouched against a garden wall not yet able to fly. I feel so much for it, this fledgling, so neatly harlequined, so almost become itself, though it would gut a nest of robins if it could. I think of the energy expended on all of it; the gestation and cracking of a blue egg, the slow feathering of a bird, and for what? Ravenous little hearts skulking in every corner, their blood thrashing around frail circulatory systems, their endings taking place out of sight.

The Scientist

XXVII

You're asking the wrong questions.
It's not what we can make,
but what we're made of.

II

But the miry places thereof and the marishes thereof shall not be healed; they shall be given to salt.

EZEKIEL 47:11

The Glacier

XXVIII

— *peekaboo*
— what was that?

The Fool

Drunk in my hotel room
I watch a documentary:

The first stars were formed!
But nobody has seen them!

In space, you can fall in any direction
so it's not really falling at all.

But from these stars came materials!
From which were built the earth!

In such a place, the faller's
agency becomes dubious.

NASA uses a space age polymer
thinner than a hair!

In space, no one can hear you.
No one can see you begin your great journey.

The drunk psychotherapist dooms you at the party

Oh borderlines are the worst, she says,
they drag everyone down with them.
I think of *Girl Interrupted* where Winona
(that is, you) was sectioned
just for just staying in bed too late
and I think, *how can you drag me down*
when you're the one who left me behind?
The therapist is swirling the dregs
of her beer in its hand-warmed bottle
and talking about manipulation, the long empty barrow
of your need. I'm picturing a grave
packed full of the tat you used to lift
from Topshop for me –
sweet-coloured bracelets,
and tubs of black eyeshadow I couldn't afford.
The psychotherapist gives me a measured look,
the one she reserves for her patients, and says:
They always kill themselves in the end.

Movie Night with Lydia

I *Beetlejuice Beetlejuice*

Between sleep and waking the TV's all blink and fizz – is this the trailer for *Beetlejuice II*? Where is Michael Keaton? The frame skips to some interdimensional scene where his gurning face emerges from a wall which probably looked spooky in 1988 but now all I can see is the poorly stippled Styrofoam and blue light through dry ice but it doesn't matter because the important thing is, he's sending hordes of the malevolent dead my way.

And the trailer is over, but the movie's still rolling and I'm in this house that seems to be a nursing home and now I have to defend it and all the smiling elderly people in their armchairs but all I have is a selection of kitchen knives – I choose the sharpest but it's one of those pronged cheese knives and is probably only sharp because who uses a cheese knife – and oh wait JEFF GOLDBLUM JEFF GOLDBLUM is in the kitchen and yeah I can see his energy working with Keaton's but he seems to be formulating some plan and too busy to tell me the details, as is the convention between men and women in movies. I wait for him to look me in the eyes and say trust me but he doesn't even.

I know the witches will come first and sure enough a rosy old lady comes along, dressed in red, holding a baby in her arms, crooning to it in a soft Baba Yaga voice. Before she can speak to me I stab her in the neck and hack her head off. It lies on the ground weeping pink jelly like that pink jelly from early Peter Jackson splatter movies before he made *LOTR* or even *Heavenly Creatures* or like the cheap fondant from the *Strawberry Dream* in a box of Cadbury's Roses. While this is happening Jeff Goldblum is still in the kitchen.

Next to arrive are three blond guys in army uniforms. The lead guy takes out a bigger knife than mine and drops it on the grass which I guess means drop mine too but I'm not participating in this particular movie trope. In he goes and it's very tense and he and Jeff Goldblum talk and then suddenly they're allies I think but I've no idea why and I wish someone could have taken five seconds to tell me this I mean I'm not an idiot and I've just slaughtered an old lady with a cheese knife.

And now I'm standing alone in the doorway of this house looking at the uranium sunlight of evening and kids playing on a swing-set oblivious to the corpse of the old lady or what the darkness might bring and I'm thinking about the *Beetlejuice* cartoon and how when I was a kid I thought Lydia and Beetlejuice were in love and maybe this, maybe this is why I'm out here alone waiting to fight a sandworm with a cheese knife while Jeff fucking Goldblum sits in the kitchen.

II *In the Neitherworld Waiting Room*

When Beetlejuice leaves the queue goes on,
snaking past the charred smoker
whose case is hardly pressing, since
you can still buy a pack of twenty
for the old money price here.
The woman with the snake
in her sleeping bag is itching
to start a conga line. The diver
with the shark bite fidgets
at the wound. Everyone feels
the press of time slipping
by in uneven increments,
its shoal buffeting them
in their seats. Harry the Hunter
is working on another scream,
but he will save it for the next aeon
in which Beetlejuice slips through
with some glamorous
newly dead or the sullen girl
who trails him now. How he'd
like to shrink that head.
And between all the rotting nuns
and dead football players with their jet-fuel char,
there sits one last living man,
forgotten by everyone, thinking
what the fuck is wrong with me
and why am i alone?

III *Jump in the Line*

Here in the group
we've all been assigned
new personalities.
Mine is 'goth who dances
to Harry Belafonte'
because it's 1988
and we don't have
manic pixie dreamgirls yet.
I still can't see my friends – a quirk of vision.
I tell the doctor:
'it's not really like
they're invisible,
it's more like
they're not actually there,' and she says:
'the reason we left
sad girl club
is that people
don't want
to spend time
with sad girls.'
After the dinner party
it's my big scene,
The one that shows I'm happy.
I hope all my friends
will be there to lift me.
It's very hot in this harness,
but if you just wait
I will levitate.

IV *Why I Won't Watch Beetlejuice Beetlejuice*

Because you know it
and I know it
both those girls
are dead

I've Been Meaning to Say, Lydia

i.m.

Lydia, it's Friday night again
        I've a naggin in my backpack
let's haunt a laneway until the rest can't put up
with our shit any more –
this is happening now, I swear it,
be here. Tonight.

*

Recurring dream
these past months
carrying you like a child
        I'm grinning   a slashed turnip
a grown woman sleeping in my arms.

*

The morning of your funeral
I perpetrate a massacre on my fingernails
with black cherry nail varnish.

It pools near my cuticles
like bruises
your poor neck –
the only thing I can think   to do:
        I'd put my cold hands on it if I could.

*

Lydia, please finish your dinner. Lydia, please drink
your tea.

*

I write a children's book for my daughter called *happy death day*.
In it two girls are twinned across time and space when one dies on
the other's birthday.

*

Lydia, if I say *no* to my second daughter
she will stop what she is doing and look at me.

    If I say *no* to my first daughter, she will never, ever stop.

*

for a moment I imagine us both sitting at your table. but inside your
kitchen cupboard is the chalk dust floor of school. and at the end of the
corridor, the stairwell where we skipped science. and in the class the
bunsen burner gifts you the flame that burns down your flat. and outside
the door are your flatmates, boyfriends, father, sister, all milling like atoms
and in the middle, a wicker coffin. I spin it all round. I can't find your
phone number. when I look out the window at the dark all I see is me.

*

Lydia, all the food in your fridge has gone bad.

*

it doesn't matter anyway
all this is just a film reel
unspooling all over the floor
when we're both gone
we can take it all back with us –
swallowing tsar bombas
with our vodkas.

*

The living girl asks the dead girl to come back
                            the dead girl ghosts her

*

hatchery of scars   tattooed over
     living craquelure   flesh animated
from chin to toe
          (your   neck)

*

Your baby's moon face radiates joy.
She's the spit of you. Her joy is the thing
that moved inside you like a snake. I never told you
the snake is what I loved, this snake
I wrapped my jealousy around.

*

my mind's eye
visits you
in your wicker bed –
soon we will not
recognise each other any more.

*

she would have had a fire in her brain he says
and I think of Yeats and his hazel wood –
    — *it's like a burning*, he says –
(golden apples)
as if I didn't know
but of course he wouldn't know I know about the wood
the smell such burning makes
she should have shown the wood
we would have known had we known
they could have known she knew about
the wood
had she shown the burning in the brain
a silver apple hovering
outside her window
moon in cooling mug

*

Lydia, where are your dogs?
        are they scratching at the door?
who has your children?
        I dream myself to your kitchen
where something moves

claw on tile
                weight of tongue slap
                on jaw
— let it out?
— let it die?

*

another house, another kitchen
        your mum pours a midday gin
tells her miscarriages like rosary beads

another house, another kitchen
        your granny passed out on the sofa
we pour a thick salt circle all over her bare floorboards

i push you and you fall backwards into it
        every time you stand up i push you again
and again i won't stop till you're safe

*

funeral fantasy: i lift your baby from your husband's arms & take her
home to where the sunlight licks the rooftiles of Edenmore, Coolock,
Kilmore, Artane & the men in the bookies wave at the women in the
beauticians & Refat in the shop gives my older daughter a lollipop &
she says, *we have a new baby!*
                & the baby smiles your smile
                        & i smile my smile
                & Refat smiles his smile

*

In the movie of the book the living girl says
I can't keep you here any more.

*

Lydia, i went back to our school.
everything had shifted 90 degrees
so all the nuns' hidden corridors
were jutting up out of the ground
and into the sky
i kept lurching sideways and the nuns
were falling up the stairs
i could hear the teeth rattle in their heads
and i wanted to shout
that you had died but knew
no one would remember your name
and oh the sun shone out of the faces
of all the happy children and
it's nice that we can visit
but now we must admit
that neither of us is ever
going home again

Lydia Reads the Cards

The Ace of Swords / The Three of Wands / The Page of Wands

They say the sky is never blue in your city,
but what if one day a giant translucent hand appears
and its sword slits the smog like an egg slicer?
What greater clarity would you want?
Go and be happy, go pretend to be happy, go find
that happiness is a full set of teeth at forty
or a tomato fucking sandwich, i don't know –
whatever your parents didn't have at your age.
Mine had what you have and called it happiness,
stuck it in photo albums, tore them up, took new photos.
Afterwards they dedicated the rest of their lives
to living longer than their parents,
and still have one full set of teeth between them.
Be the boy with the brightest teeth. Be the oldest teenager.
But don't make this floating sword the elephant in your room.
We can all see it and we know it's yours.

Entre des bois et des plages sauvages

is the name of the trail I run
not really knowing my way back
to the chalet where my husband and children sit
not knowing where I am either.
At the top I turn, look at the sea and think
how convenient the way the tides
take the bodies away
how convenient for some.
The sea is a blue too lazy to match the sky
which, in any case, is grey,
and I am about to chance my arm for another decade –
offer limb after limb to the sea,
while my husband and children
sit in their brightly lit chalet
no body running the wooded path back to them.

Tiger

When the tiger comes to tea
and eats all your sandwiches
the unspoken rule is
you can't ask him to leave
until the devastation is complete –
till he's eaten all the packages in the cupboard
and worse
drunk all daddy's beer.
But the child in your kitchen
keeps running to him,
twining his tail
round her neck –
boa snake scarf –
and you wonder
what will he do to her
if you tell him he has to go.

Putting My Arms Around the Goat

> And then I hear a little bell and go up to the attic
> and put my arms around a goat
>
> MARY RUEFLE

Maybe I imagined you. It's possible.
My thoughts of you fold you inside me
like three children in a trench coat.
Your violent wobble. Your little horns –
these things I see that may not be real
at all. Damp illusions with which
I try to keep warm. This sodden sweater
I keep getting tangled up in. Look,
I'm struggling out of one sleeve, look,
I'm reaching for you. I'd happily snip
every garland I've wound around your neck.
I'll put my arms around what's left. Even
if you kick. Even if you bolt.

In the Night Garden

My daughter is in the Night Garden again.
It's a metaphor, I say to my husband –
the boy stranded on a boat in the dark ocean,
falling into a sleep that's surely death
and the last thing he sees is a garden
where he can play with his friends
and be put to bed and wake up again
in the same dapple of sun,
the only thing lost being time.
Isn't that what you would want? I ask him,
to lose nothing from this world but the time
that strips everything away? I'm crying now –
I go into the kitchen so as not to upset my daughter
who is standing watching *Iggle Piggle*,
the only child not yet in bed.

A kid tells my daughter her storybook is broken

Yes, bits of it are torn
because we rescued it
from a box of rain-drenched books
left orphaned on the pavement.
I wouldn't have bought
this weird *Red Riding Hood*
with its holographic insets
or chosen a version where it says
the granny was gobbled up by the wolf,
then cut out of his belly.
When I read it I have to substitute
the wolf locked the granny in the wardrobe
and instead of the Woodsman
freeing the granny in a slither
of entrails I say: *They put the wolf in jail!*,
because I can tell my kid is afraid of
and compelled by the wolf
like all kids are compelled by, afraid of
the blade the needle the bottle with its skull and cross bones the
thundering wheels of trucks the electric fence you might just grab –
and I want to be my daughter's safety in that place
not some blindfolded Justice juggling kitchen implements –
so yes, our storybook is
torn and full of gaudy foil,
but Jesus, look around you,
at the boiling sky and dog shit pavements,
at the glimmer bleeding from the light's edge.

Allegory

After Caravaggio's The Taking of Christ

Walking in the National Gallery with A,
she says, that's Jesus. He was nailed to a cross.
We pass so many naked Jesuses.
I want to say to her, it's allegory
but she is five and so I wonder
what it means to her, all these muscled
old men in loincloths
and youthful Marys cradling corpses –
Jesus stretched like a skinned rabbit.
We go back to *The Taking of Christ.*
She asks, why does Jesus look like that
and I say he's sad because he's been betrayed
and she says why was he betrayed
which makes me think of the whole pantomime
of his choosing death when he knew
it wasn't really death
and I'm not sure I can explain betrayal at all.
So instead I reach into the painting
swing the guard's lantern
until all the men's faces are in shadow
and there's the shape of a door in the wall.

Villanelle Villanelle

'Your eyes will just empty. Your soul goes in... It falls so far in
it just becomes so small that it can't control your body any more.
It's just in there, tiny forever.'

VILLANELLE, *Killing Eve*

Your eyes just empty. Your soul goes in,
back to the hive that once housed it.
It falls so far it can't control your body.

And when you drop your cutlery and stand
on the table in your own small kitchen,
your eyes just empty. Your soul goes in,

swims away from me. And picking it up
would be like scooping water through my fingers –
it falls so far it can't control your body

and you were always too heavy for me to lift.
I'd watch you trace your ribcage with your fingers,
how your eyes would just empty. Your soul gone in

behind those bars, and everyone watching a girl
stumble off a table. The arches of your feet
fallen, too weak to hold your body –

but the drop is your choice. The drop takes choice away.
Let me fold you like a towel on some warm shelf
while your eyes empty. I'll tuck your soul in
when it becomes so small it can't control your body.

The Keeners

What better job for the living, Lydia,
then to cry for those who stumbled
into death's confusing age-long blink?
What the fuck, they are thinking,
swimming circles in the blackness, *what the fuck*,
while we sit here above them,
leaking saltwater that rises up around their gills.
We are feeling all our feelings,
new dilations occurring to admit more sensibility.
That's where the life force is Lydia, in this opening inward,
in this useless spelunking – no matter how deep we go,
we won't reach you.

I Read the Cards

The Seven of Wands / The Moon / Temperance

Moon, show me this man's wandering orbit.
Light up the dirt I've nestled in my ribcage
allow me to finger it open,
salvage, at least, some seeds.
Once I was a dummy with a stave across my gut.
Once I was so ready to be hit I'd put on different shoes,
I'd pull up every sapling just to avoid getting lost in the woods.
But now I'm a crayfish in a world of dogs
crawling up a sky as smooth as my lizard brain.
Once I get my pincers hooked on that air
I'll grow my wings and be the happy angel, I swear it,
pouring my wine from cup to cup and never blackening my lips.

The Thief

XXIX

While you were sleeping
I took:
a page from every
one of your books
your full stops
all the green letters
from your name

what the women are doing

(for Elaine Feeney)

while we watch our movies sunk in beanbags
    the women
are talking without pause of yogurts and blocked guts
    ladling food into handbags
        where it settles in sediments that birth
flourishing ecosystems.
They look up, these tiny species,
    call *mother* to the sky – and it's true
    the women will always be more mother than they might choose
      – the snare of mother, the trap, the body's gibbet post –
    Heedless above these worlds, the women
  are talking, great fish bowls of wine
pivoting on gold-laced wrists,
    talking about, no – not figs or pomegranates,
but raisins, prunes, the consolation of dried physallis and patience,
    how they rattle in the quiet hours.
  And as we stuff our faces with popcorn, chomp milk teeth,
they are talking, of course,
    about what can be thinned to secrecy,
        and taken with them in the night.

Junk File of Incorrect Predictions

I pulled a card   then another   then another   then another until the whole deck formed a mosaic spelling out: *you should keep going* even though you're standing naked in front of an angel and what do you think that angel will say? and so I pulled the guts from a pigeon and tried to read them, slapping its small intestine onto the ground and asking *what's my true love's name? what's my true love's name?* but all it said was *pain pain pain* and I got on the bus to town to drown out the sound of birdsong and the bus stopped outside *pain quotidien* and so I asked the barista what he knew about everyday pain and only then did I remember I hadn't dressed myself and people in the shop kept saying *you're getting so thin* as if I had ever dared to fill more space than the bare minimum. So I took my bare minimum back outside and ran home on all fours because it's quicker that way, and the angel is coming to take all the rotten bodies and put them together, after all these years, and will they be happy to see their old arms and legs? Will they be happy to see their old husbands and wives? And the cards told me the man was just afraid to lose his coins, and the cards told me his staff was sprouting a pristine bud, but they didn't mention that I'm nothing but a barking dog. And the tea leaves showed me a soldier, a sailor, a candlestick maker, but those jobs don't exist any more. The crystal ball promised travel, before I dropped it on my foot and the Magic 8 Ball keeps saying *all signs point to no*. But the cards say everything is fine,

    and it will be fine

if fine is a tangle of guts

        and a woman

           on all fours, howling.

The Algorithm

XXX

Behold my cursed Instagram reels:
a little girl kisses her twin,
but her sister has only half a head.
A premature baby, all mottled veins
and bulging eyes flails weakly,
hair stood on end like a cadaver.

And everyone says

but you asked for this

you must have

you wanted it

you asked

Rabbits

My girls in the garden
in their underwear,

skin pinked by sun.
Twitch and flinch

of hair that skims
their shoulders;

in a rabbit's flight,
half-seen.

Mist harvesters –
Nothing so soft or aimless.

Bodies stretched
as if still running.

Stripped of fur, flesh-gleam
like human skin glazed in sweat,

flayed and kinked
as a used tampon.

Thin pickings.
Proof of life.

The Good Girls

XXXI

are taking care of history –
they close their eyes so tight
they've tunnelled right through
to the backs of their heads.

One day I'll lie down
have my face washed clean
and say sorrysorrysorry
for all the things I've seen.

The Steak

Dark marbled char, flesh-pink, air dried,
sweetened with maggot bites.
Is the steak worth the money
I wonder as a peppercorn lodges
in my molar like a mortar.
Is my time worth the money I am paid
and what meat is being sliced elsewhere;
what is meat's worth?
In the meeting earlier, a man had said –
Her feet, her feet were gone, and if her mother let her fall –
and no one seemed to know
how to stop him talking.
It is a good thing, I think,
that we can't fully arrest misery
before it throttles us.
I keep chewing my steak.
I keep swallowing.

The nights I don't think about you

are more frequent. This
is one of them. The hallway
has sprouted one hundred new doors
and I realise I haven't opened
any. You could only be inside
one, of course. Maybe with
your back turned, the nape of your neck
exposed. But I keep walking,
up the stairs and into the bathroom
where I greet only myself.
I wash my hands for the allotted time.
When they're slick enough,
I mould shreds of soap into likenesses
that aren't yours and I am soothed –
my palms slipping their itch.

Parachute Malfunction

Trying to reason with myself that what I feel is the re-emergence of
    buried self-loathing and not that other thing
but when I crack my ribcage for you and my lungs flair out like silk,
lift me from the ground,
how can this not be love?

Always Eating Your Dad

Mine was a mine fantasia, I say,
    to which he replies, *what?*
I clarify: as in his tomb the mine, my gift to him a well filled with rusted
    cars
...(I'm losing him now)
And yours!, I say, Still alive but you, you build him profiterole Taj Mahals! –
his face memorialised in plaited breads,
composed of sliced meats in quivering aspic domes.
    Look! He's shaped from reconstituted salmon
        a merman tailed with cucumber scales –
how beautiful, these patriarchal canapes,
    his fingers as iced biscuits, his eyes thin-sliced radishes
        blotted with caviar –
o take this and eat of it –
    but (and here I pause) can I ask why, though?
    is it because you are afraid you might turn into him?
    No that's not the problem, he says –
you see
    I can't turn into anyone.

King of Wands (Reversed)

The thought struck me –
after all this time, why not
write you a love poem?
So I turned you upside down
and shook until all the adders
you'd hidden up your sleeves
hit the ground and coiled away.
I'm still shaking, but the nothing
that falls out now looks like grief.
If you could hear me I'd ask you
to take off your clothes
and stand very close to me.
Be quiet though, your words are useless.
Even the ones I imagine are insults.
I can't look inside you,
but when I look inside me
every organ's scorched clean.
I wanted the honesty of your body,
I wanted to interrogate it with my own.
Here are your snakes.
Here is your love poem.

The New Moon

XXX

And so I choose my moon;
his light just strong enough
to silver my ridges and craters,
to lick my dust oceans to life.
Our proximity gives us
both this Kodachrome glamour –
if he likes the gift, I can't tell,
but here he comes again
waxing, his close orbit.
Quiet friend, I say, I'll turn
every mirror in my house towards you.

Well-behaved

The dead are well-behaved, aren't they Lydia?
        They contort right into any box you open for them
then pop out again, faces washed clean.

The living can gift them little mermaid voices
        and call them flowers upon the winter heath.
We can't give them back their blood though,
        or their mucus or their cum.

We can't give them back a single thought,
        though we have many thoughts about them –
they must suffer our thoughts in silence.

A reading for the dead

I could have picked up the phone,
lit a candle, moved a glass
across the board to summon you,

instead, I pull three cards.
They're blank, edges charred,
but they fall just as heavy.

You're out there in the bay –
your husband is punting you into the sea's mouth.
Your babies are with you too.

You crawled under the laminate
long before you died.
You left me first and I
was too proud to cry.

to you, one year on

your missed voice call still listed
the video you'd sent   clouded   waiting
     for something to set it in motion

spring juddering to life in fits   and   starts
     a body that's taken too much punishment
i lie in my hospital bed   wellspring of amniotic fluid

since the induction began   waters pooling here
below the dublin mountains
      riding the liffey to the coast

the baby comes   and elsewhere   you go
i think of the sea   hunched at clontarf
     tides paused to let you both pass

the rivers have gone   now   the blood
     so i walk the halls   legs heavy
i think about you   write you a message
     hold your lost property   for a year and a day

Ten of Swords

And when the worst happens
you are cleansed. A morning street free
of crowds. A fox on the roadside
pulverised to purity. Red fur shake.
A room with every surface slick
and rippling. An empty ward with all
catastrophes wheeled away – listen, can
you hear the echo? Whittled bone clean,
thinned past texture, fractal fine.
The dander in the feather, the crouching mite.
A morning paused always just before sunrise.
Ten swords pierce you, and you're doing all right.

lydia...

i asked the internet what it felt like

         and it just gave me the samaritans hotline. see,

i'm checking in on you. i never stopped.

i'm a cloud on a backdrop.

        someone painted me here. i had to have,

in the moment of my conception,

        some utility.

On Halloween

Love, earlier I'd thought
the dead were playing tricks on us
when in my rush to reach you
I fell up our stairs,
bruised ogham-lines
across my shins.
But in our bedroom I know
we're playing tricks on them –
open in me the eye
that shows me forgotten things:
indigo fog over Mountjoy Square,
the yellow of a night-time train station,
the red airborne shape of a slap
I once felt a woman give me
seven leagues away.
I offer it back to you, dead billions,
in your sleeping rows –
the open lens,
the wash of it,
the seas' Caesarean fold where riptides meet.
What does the cell know
as it swims in the Petri dish?
I know points of light, I know laughter.
My flesh and my closest flesh
are laughing at you still.

ACKNOWLEDGEMENTS & NOTES

ACKNOWLEDGEMENTS

Thanks to the editors of the following journals in which many of these poems have appeared: 'Becoming Schrodinger's Cat' appeared in *Bad Lilies*; 'On Halloween' appeared in *Basket Magazine*; 'Putting My Arms Around the Goat' appeared in *bath magg*; 'Entre des bois et des plages sauvages', 'The Prize', 'Magpie Heart', 'Raptured' and 'A kid tells my daughter her storybook is broken' appeared in *Berlin Lit*; 'Allegory', 'Villanelle Villanelle', 'Roger Moore's Swimming Pool' and 'The drunk psychotherapist dooms you at the party' appeared in *Hog River Press*; 'Minor Complaints' appeared in *The London Magazine*; 'I'm Quartered' appeared in *Magma*; 'The Nights I Don't Think About You' and 'Lydia...' appeared in *Poetry London*; 'monstera' 'I'm lydia deetz and all my friends are dead' and 'and the girl inside me' appeared in *The Poetry Review*; 'to you, one year on' appeared in *New England Review*; 'Mean/Meant Aubade' appeared in *Ploughshares*; 'Movie Night with Lydia' was featured on the RTÉ Culture page for Culture Night 2024, and 'what the women are doing' appeared in *Zocalo Public Square*.

'Sheila on the Red Bed' was written in response to an invitation by the Hugh Lane Gallery to contribute to a panel discussion on their 2022 Patrick Graham retrospective. 'Bog Virgin' was written in response to an invitation by The Abbey Theatre and Inua Ellams to respond to Neil Jordan's film adaptation of Pat McCabe's *The Butcher Boy* for Poetry + Film Hack at the Irish Film Institute in 2022.

Many of these poems were written during my time as Yeats Society Sligo poet in residence in 2020-22, DLR poet-in-residence in 2022, as Arts Council writer in residence at Galway University in 2023, and at the Culture Ireland/Literature Ireland Literarisches Colloquium Berlin residency as part of Zeitgeist 24 in 2024; my lasting thanks to all involved in these residencies and for the space and time they gave me to create. I am grateful to the Arts Council of Ireland for a Literature Bursary in 2024 which gave me time to edit this collection.

THANKS

To Declan, Abigail, Isobel, and my parents Billie and Anthony for being the source of all my happiness. To the wonderful Elaine Feeney for being the source of all my sanity. To Jane Clarke, Eithne Hand, Rosamund Taylor and Simon Costello for always being my first and best readers. To Sinéad Gleeson, Victoria Kennefick, Seán Hewitt, Adam Wyeth, Conor O'Callaghan and Stephen Sexton for being great friends and fellow travellers. To my fellow Banshees Laura Jane Cassidy and Eimear Ryan, and to our brilliant Banshee poets – Bebe Ashley, Rosamund Taylor (again!), Dylan Brennan and Gustav Parker Hibbett. To the wonderful Lisa Sterle who created the cover image for this collection, which I will treasure forever. To Neil Astley and all at Bloodaxe for the editorial insight and support. To my many, many other friends and companions in the writing community – you are too many to name here, but thank you always for your friendship, empathy, and humour.

Finally – to Lydia, and our youth.

NOTES

The small poems numbered from XXIII to XXXII are ideas for a New Arcana, continuing where the Major Arcana of the tarot leaves off.

The poems in the first 'Movie Night with Lydia' sequence reference Tim Burton's 1992 movie *Batman Returns*.

The poems in the second 'Movie Night with Lydia' sequence respond to Tim Burton's 1988 film *Beetlejuice*. 'Jump in the Line' by Harry Belafonte is the song played in the movie's final scene, where Lydia Deetz levitates.